Book bri...

1 Set in modern times, it tells the story of Lizzie's very different summer in the countryside of Yorkshire, England.

2 Lizzie, almost 15 years old, is furious when she finds out she can't spend the summer with her friends in Blackpool.

3 Lizzie's first meeting with Hannah confirms all Lizzie's fears that this is going to be the worst summer of her life.

4 Then Lizzie meets Jack, a strange boy with a red balloon and things start to change.

5 Main themes include growing up, friendship, love and mystery.

www.eligradedreaders.com

In this reader:

 **21st Century Skills** — To encourage students to connect the story to the world they live in.

Key — A2 level activities.

Story Notes — A brief summary of the text.

Glossary — Explanation of difficult words.

Picture Caption — A brief explanation of the picture.

Audio — These icons indicate the parts of the story that are recorded. ▶ start ■ stop

Think — To encourage students to develop their critical thinking skills.

Silvana Sardi

The Boy with the Red Balloon

Illustrated by
Maria Girón

Teen ELi Readers

Teen Eli Readers

The **ELI Readers** collection is a complete range of books and plays for readers of all ages, ranging from captivating contemporary stories to timeless classics. There are four series, each catering for a different age group: **First ELI Readers, Young ELI Readers, Teen ELI Readers** and **Young Adult ELI Readers**. The books are carefully edited and beautifully illustrated to capture the essence of the stories and plots. The readers are supplemented with 'Focus on' texts packed with background cultural information about the writers and their lives and times.

The Boy with the Red Balloon
by **Silvana Sardi**
Illustrated by **Maria Girón**
Language Level Consultant
Lisa Suett

ELI Readers
Founder and Series Editors
Paola Accattoli, Grazia Ancillani, Daniele Garbuglia (Art Director)

Graphic Design
**Andersen
the Premedia Company**

Production Manager
Francesco Capitano

Photo credits
Shutterstock

New edition: **2021**
First edition: **2017**

© ELI s.r.l.
P.O. Box 6
62019 Recanati MC
Italy
T +39 071750701
F +39 071977851
info@elionline.com
www.elionline.com

Typeset in 12 / 17 pt
Fulmar designed by Leo Philp

Printed in Italy by
**Tecnostampa - Pigini Group
Printing Division
Loreto - Trevi
ERT 252.10
ISBN 978-88-536-3204-3**

Contents

6	**Main Characters**	
8	**Before you read**	
10	**Chapter 1**	*A Different Summer*
18	**Activities**	
20	**Chapter 2**	*Goodbye Blackpool*
28	**Activities**	
30	**Chapter 3**	*A Strange Meeting in the Woods*
42	**Activities**	
44	**Chapter 4**	*Summer Love*
52	**Activities**	
54	**Chapter 5**	*The Lake*
62	**Activities**	
64	**Chapter 6**	*Past Meets Present*
72	**Activities**	
74	**Focus on...**	*Blackpool*
76	**Focus on...**	*Strange Stories*
78	**Test Yourself**	
79	**Syllabus**	

Before you read

Reading A2 Key

① Complete the text about the book with one word in each space.

This story is about a girl called Lizzie __who__ comes from Blackpool, a town near the sea in northwest England. Lizzie is happy (**1**) _____ the summer holidays have arrived and she can go to the beach and have fun (**2**) _____ her friends. She doesn't know that this summer (**3**) _____ be different. She has to go and stay with (**4**) _____ mum's friend in the Yorkshire countryside, far from everyone and everything she knows. Lizzie is (**5**) _____ angry with her parents because she's going to miss all the summer fun. Then she meets a strange boy with a red balloon and (**6**) _____ countryside suddenly becomes more interesting.

Speaking and Writing

21st Century Skills

② At the start of the story, Lizzie is excited because school has just finished for the summer.
Discuss these questions with a partner and write your answers.

1 When does your school finish for the summer holidays?
2 How long is the summer break from school where you live?
3 Do you usually see your classmates during the summer holidays? Why? / Why not?
4 What do you usually do during the summer break?
5 Do you prefer going to the mountains or the beach when you go on holiday with your family?
6 Which famous city would you like to visit?

Listening A2 Key

▶ 2 ❸ **Listen to the start of Chapter 1 and choose the correct answer (A, B or C).**

   Lizzie and her friends
   - **A** ☐ ran to the beach.
   - **B** ☐ ran to school.
   - **C** ☑ ran out of the classroom.

1. It was the start of the
   - **A** ☐ summer holidays.
   - **B** ☐ Easter holidays.
   - **C** ☐ Christmas holidays.

2. Lizzie is
   - **A** ☐ the same age as Greg.
   - **B** ☐ two years older than Greg.
   - **C** ☐ two years younger than Greg.

3. Lizzie has
   - **A** ☐ long, red hair.
   - **B** ☐ short, fair hair.
   - **C** ☐ long, dark hair.

4. Lizzie went home
   - **A** ☐ by car.
   - **B** ☐ on foot.
   - **C** ☐ by bus.

5. It took Lizzie
   - **A** ☐ twelve minutes to get home.
   - **B** ☐ two minutes to get home.
   - **C** ☐ twenty minutes to get home.

6. That day it was
   - **A** ☐ cloudy.
   - **B** ☐ quite hot.
   - **C** ☐ quite cold.

7. Lizzie won't be at school in
   - **A** ☐ August.
   - **B** ☐ September.
   - **C** ☐ June.

Chapter 1

A Different Summer

▶ 2 DRRRING! The school bell rang. 'Hooray!' Lizzie and her friends ran out of the classroom shouting and laughing. It was the last day of school! Summer was here! It was time for the beach! Time for fun!

'Bye Lizzie! See you later!'

Lizzie turned when she heard her name. It was Greg! Greg was seventeen, two years older than she was. She really liked him. He was tall, with short, fair hair and brown eyes. He was really cool. All the girls liked him.

'Hi, I mean, bye Greg!' she said.

Her heart went boom, boom, boom! It happened every time she spoke to him. And her face … it was as red as her long, red hair! Greg smiled, then got on his bike and rode away. Lizzie watched until he turned the corner. *Maybe we can go for a ride together during the summer holidays,* she thought.

Lizzie started to walk home. It took her twenty minutes but she didn't mind. It was warm and

Lizzie and her friends are all happy that school has finished for the summer holidays. Lizzie really likes Greg, a boy at school, and she hopes they can maybe go for a ride on their bikes together during the summer holidays.

❯ Lizzie is walking home from school and thinking about all the nice things she's going to do during the summer holidays.

Silvana Sardi

sunny and she had time to think. No more school uniform… no more exams… it was the end of July and school didn't start again until the beginning of September! Then there was Greg.

I've never had a real boyfriend, she thought. *Maybe this summer will be different!*

▶ 3

Lizzie thinks about all the nice things she can do that summer, but when she arrives home her mum and dad want to talk to her. She's worried because her mum calls her 'Elizabeth' and she only ever does that when she's not pleased with Elizabeth.

Lizzie loved Blackpool, especially[1] in summer. There was so much to do. She wanted to go to the beach. She wanted to go up Blackpool Tower … the view was great up there. She wanted to have a picnic with her friends in Stanley Park. Then there was the 'Lights Festival'. It was always fantastic!

'Hi, Mum! Hi, Dad!' shouted Lizzie as she came into the house.

'Elizabeth,' said her mum, 'come into the living room. Your dad and I need to talk to you.'

Uh-oh, what have I done now? thought Lizzie. Her mum only called her 'Elizabeth' when there was a problem. She walked slowly into the room. Her mum and dad were sitting on the sofa.

'What's the matter?' asked Lizzie.

'How was your last day of school?' asked her dad.

---

[1] **especially** above all

The Boy with the Red Balloon

'Great!' said Lizzie. 'We're all really excited about going to the beach and …'

'Listen,' said her mum, 'I know you're not going to like this Lizzie, but there's nothing we can do …'

'What won't I like?' asked Lizzie, now very worried.

'Tomorrow you're leaving for Yorkshire to stay with my old school friend, Hannah, for the summer,' her mum said quickly.

'What?' shouted Lizzie. 'Yorkshire! What do you mean? Is this some kind of bad joke[1]?'

'I'm afraid not,' said her dad.

'But what have I done? Why are you doing this to me?' said Lizzie almost in tears[2].

'I'm sorry Lizzie,' said her dad. 'Do you remember last winter when there was the terrible storm?'

'Yes,' said Lizzie, 'and our house was flooded[3] like everybody's house in the street, but …'

'Well,' said her dad, 'this morning a man came to look at the house. He told us that the roof isn't safe and we need a new one. It's a big job Lizzie,

> Lizzie can't believe it and almost cries when her mum says she has to go and stay in Yorkshire for the summer. She doesn't understand why they're doing this to her.

---

[1] **bad joke** a joke that isn't funny
[2] **in tears** crying
[3] **flooded** full of water

Silvana Sardi

and we can't stay here while they're working on it. We need to do it now before next winter.'

'But what about you and Mum?' asked Lizzie. 'What are you going to do?'

'Your mum and I need to stay near home so we can go to work. We're going to stay, in a caravan¹. A man from work has one. He says we can use it until the house is ready.'

'Well, I can stay in the caravan too!' said Lizzie.

'You can't, it's too small,' said her mum. 'There's only one bed.'

'I don't mind,' said Lizzie. 'I'll sleep on the floor! Please don't send me away! I want to stay here with my friends … and you!'

'Oh Lizzie, darling,' said her mum, 'it's not just the caravan. Your dad and I will be at work every night. After working at the supermarket, I'm going to work as a waitress in a restaurant to make some more money. And your dad has asked his boss at work for all the overtime² he can give him. This roof job is going to cost a lot of money.'

Lizzie looked at her mum and dad. She felt sorry for them, but she felt even sorrier for

> The family can't stay in the house while the men are working on the roof. The caravan is only big enough for Lizzie's parents who have to stay near home for work. They also need to work longer hours to pay for the roof job.

¹ **caravan**
² **overtime** extra hours you work

The Boy with the Red Balloon

herself. Then she had an idea.

'Why can't I stay with Rachel? She's my best friend. I've stayed with her before. Her mum won't mind.'

'No, Lizzie,' said her father. 'It's one thing staying the night, but you can't stay with them for the whole summer.'

'The WHOLE summer?' shouted Lizzie. 'Do you mean I need to stay with this Hannah woman for the WHOLE summer?'

'Well, we don't know yet,' said her mum, 'but it's a big job. Anyway, Hannah is one of my oldest friends. She's really nice. I'm sure you'll like her. There's nobody else. You've only got one uncle and he lives in Australia … a bit too far, eh?' said her mum trying to smile.

'But I don't even know this friend of yours. I don't think I've ever met her,' said Lizzie.

'I've known Hannah since we were at school,' said her mum. 'The last time you saw her, you were just a baby. That's why you don't remember.'

Sara Hammond looked at her husband and

Lizzie may have to stay with Hannah for the whole summer and she can't even remember meeting her.

Silvana Sardi

for a moment, nobody spoke. They were both thinking about that particular day in August. Such a sad time for Hannah. But Lizzie didn't know anything about that and Sara wasn't going to tell her now.

Lizzie looked at them both. She could tell there was something wrong.

'So why haven't I seen her since then?' she asked.

'Hannah is a very quiet person and she likes to be by herself in the countryside,' said her mum.

'Oh, great!' shouted Lizzie. 'You're sending me to live with a hermit[1]! The countryside! I hate the countryside! What am I going to do there? Play with the sheep and cows? Swim with the ducks?'

'That's enough, Elizabeth!' said her dad. He was starting to get angry now. 'You're not the only one who's going to have a 'different' summer!'

He stood up and walked out of the room. Lizzie looked at her mum.

'Lizzie, don't worry,' said her mum. 'Hannah isn't that bad. I'm sure she'll take you to York to do some shopping. It's a lovely city…'

Lizzie thinks it's strange that she hasn't seen this woman since she was a baby if she's such a good friend of her mum. Her mum says Hannah is very quiet and lives in the countryside. When Lizzie hears that she feels even angrier than before.

---

[1] **hermit** a person who lives a simple life a long way from other people

The Boy with the Red Balloon

'But I don't want to go to York!' shouted Lizzie. 'I don't know anyone in York! I want to be with my friends here in Blackpool!'

Lizzie ran out of the room and upstairs to her bedroom. She threw herself on the bed and cried and cried. She didn't go down for dinner that evening. She texted all her friends and told them the bad news. They all felt sorry for her. Greg's message said: *'Hey! What a pity! Have fun anyway!!* ☺*'*

Have fun? The second bad joke of the day, thought Lizzie. He was going to have fun for sure and she already knew who with … Jenny! Jenny was a girl in her class at school and she really fancied[1] Greg. *She won't waste time,* thought Lizzie. *She'll have Greg all to herself and I can't do anything about it!* Lizzie started to cry again. She was going to hate every minute of this summer, she thought as she fell asleep[2] that night. ⬛

> Lizzie is so sad and angry that she cries herself to sleep, especially at the thought that another girl at her school called Jenny will try to become Greg's girlfriend and Lizzie won't be there to stop her.

> **Think**
> Lizzie is very angry with her parents. Do you ever feel like this?

[1] **fancy** when you want someone to be your girlfriend / boyfriend
[2] **fall asleep** go to sleep

After-reading Activities • Chapter 1

Reading Comprehension

1 **Read the sentences about Chapter 1 and decide if they are true (T) or false (F).**

		T	F
	Lizzie is sad because school has finished.	☐	✓
1	She goes home with a friend.	☐	☐
2	Her mum and dad are in the kitchen.	☐	☐
3	The roof of the house is dangerous.	☐	☐
4	Her mum and dad are going to stay with friends.	☐	☐
5	Hannah lives in the countryside.	☐	☐
6	Lizzie knows Hannah very well.	☐	☐

Grammar

2 **Complete the questions with a word from the box, then match them with the right answer.**

> ~~Who~~   Who   Where   When
> Why   What   Whose

b	_Who_	does Lizzie like?
1	_____	is Lizzie's best friend?
2	_____	does Lizzie want to do in Stanley Park?
3	_____	does she need to leave for Yorkshire?
4	_____	must her parents work harder than usual?
5	_____	are her parents going to stay this summer?
6	_____	house is Lizzie going to stay in?

a   Hannah's.
b ✓ Greg.
c   Have a picnic.
d   The day after.
e   To pay for the new roof.
f   Rachel.
g   In a caravan.

Speaking

21st Century Skills

3 Look at the picture again of Lizzie walking home from school and discuss these questions with a partner.

1 Lizzie is wearing a school uniform. What do you wear to school?
2 Do you think all students should wear a school uniform? Why? / Why not?
3 Lizzie is walking home from school. How do you usually get home from school?
4 How long does it take you to get to school in the morning? Why?
5 Do you ever ride your bike to school? Why? / Why not?
6 How important is it for people to use their cars less? Why?

Before-reading Activity

Listening A2 Key

▶ 4 **4 Listen to the start of Chapter 2 and complete the sentences.**

Next morning it was ___*cloudy*___ .
1 Lizzie found her _____ in a drawer.
2 Lizzie's mum wanted to help her with her _____ .
3 That morning for breakfast, there was sausage, bacon and _____ .
4 Lizzie had breakfast with her mum and _____ .
5 Lizzie's train was at half past _____ .
6 Lizzie is going to take some old _____ with her.
7 Lizzie went _____ to finish packing her bag.

Chapter 2

Goodbye Blackpool

▶ 4 Next morning when Lizzie woke up it was cloudy. *Fantastic! Just what I needed,* thought Lizzie. She opened a drawer and started to pull out some things to take with her. She stopped when she saw her new bikini. Her mum came into the room.

'Lizzie, are you OK? Come and have some breakfast and then I'll help you with your bag.'

'Well, I don't think I'll need this,' said Lizzie holding up the new bikini.

'Oh, Lizzie!' said her mum. 'I know it's hard for you, but try to understand.'

'I know, I know,' said Lizzie.

They went downstairs for breakfast. Lizzie's dad was there too.

'Your mum has made your favourite, Lizzie,' he said. 'Sausage, bacon and eggs!'

Lizzie said nothing. She sat down at the table. She pushed her food around her plate. She didn't eat much.

Mr and Mrs Hammond looked at each other. They loved their daughter very much. They hated seeing her like this.

Lizzie finds her new bikini in her drawer. She won't need that in the countryside. Her mum has made her favourite breakfast for her but Lizzie is too upset to eat it all.

The Boy with the Red Balloon

'The train is at half past eleven, Lizzie,' said her dad. 'Are you almost ready to go?'

'Yes,' said Lizzie quietly. 'I just need to put a few old T-shirts in my bag. I won't need any of my new summer stuff¹ where I'm going.'

'I'll come and help you,' said her mum.

'No, it's alright. I'll do it myself,' said Lizzie.

She stood up and went upstairs to finish packing.

▶ 5 'I hope she'll be alright, John,' said Mrs Hammond to her husband.

'I'm sure she will,' said Mr Hammond. 'You know, Lizzie, she's a good girl. She's just angry at the moment but it'll pass. Hannah will be nice to her.'

'Yes,' said his wife. 'I spoke to Hannah yesterday. She said she'll look after her. But I'm worried. We both know how much Hannah has suffered² and summer is the worst time for her. I hope Lizzie doesn't find things difficult there.'

'Maybe she'll help Hannah to be happy again,' said Mr Hammond.

'Maybe …' she answered. 'Right, I'll go and see if Lizzie is ready. It's time to go.'

Lizzie's parents talk about Hannah while Lizzie is upstairs. Hannah has suffered a lot and summer is the worst time for her, so Lizzie's mum is worried that Lizzie may find things difficult at Hannah's.

---

¹ **stuff** things
² **suffer** when you feel very sad about something

Silvana Sardi

Nobody spoke as they drove to the train station. The train was already waiting on the platform¹ when they arrived. Lizzie kissed her parents quickly.

'Take care, Lizzie,' said Mrs Hammond. 'Hannah will be at York Station to meet you.'

'OK,' was all Lizzie said. She got on the train and found her seat. Her parents stood on the platform until the train disappeared².

Lizzie looked out of the window of the train. She felt empty inside. *Goodbye Blackpool, goodbye friends, goodbye summer fun*, she thought.

Three long hours passed. Finally, the train arrived in York. She got off and looked around. Then someone called her name.

'Elizabeth?'

In front of her was a thin woman in her forties³. She was wearing an old, dark grey tracksuit⁴. She had long hair, more grey than blond.

'Yes,' said Lizzie. She felt a bit afraid. There was something sad in the woman's big green eyes. Her

Lizzie's dad says that maybe Lizzie will help Hannah to be happy again.

Nobody says anything on the way to the station. Lizzie kisses her parents quickly and gets on the train. She feels really empty inside. Hannah is waiting for her at York station.

Lizzie is on the train to York station. She feels really empty inside at the thought of not spending the summer with her friends in Blackpool.

¹ **platform** where people wait for a train
² **disappear** go out of view
³ **in her forties** between 40 and 49 years old
⁴ **tracksuit** trousers and jacket people wear for sport

Silvana Sardi

face was pale[1] and thin. *Oh dear! Is she ill? Why's she so sad?* thought Lizzie.

'Hi, I'm Hannah,' said the woman. 'Come on, the car's in front of the station.'

Then she turned and started walking towards the exit. Lizzie stood for a moment and then quickly followed her.

They drove for an hour along the main[2] road. It was the longest hour in Lizzie's life. Hannah said nothing and Lizzie was too scared[3] to say anything. Then they came to a smaller country road. They drove past fields and trees, and more fields and more trees. *No town,* thought Lizzie, *no shops … nothing!* Just a few farmhouses. Lizzie wanted to cry. This was going to be the worst summer of her life!

After about half an hour, Hannah stopped the car in front of a grey cottage[4].

'Here we are,' she said. 'Get your stuff and I'll show you your room.'

Lizzie got out of the car and looked around.

Hannah has sad eyes and Lizzie feels a bit scared of her. Hannah says nothing in the car and all Lizzie can see are fields and trees. She's sure this is going to be the worst summer of her life.

Hannah's cottage in the middle of the countryside where there are only fields and trees all around.

[1] **pale** white
[2] **main** big, important
[3] **scared** afraid
[4] **cottage** a house in the country

Silvana Sardi

> Lizzie doesn't know what she's going to do all summer in the middle of the countryside. At least her bedroom is nice. Actually this room is much nicer than all the others. For a moment Hannah looks happier when Lizzie says the room is lovely.

There was a garden in front of the cottage. There was the cottage ... and then? Nothing! They were in the middle of the countryside! *I don't believe it!* thought Lizzie. *What am I going to do here?*

'Elizabeth! Come on!' shouted Hannah.

'Coming!' answered Lizzie.

'So, this is my house,' said Hannah. They were standing in the kitchen. 'The living room is there,' she said pointing to a door across the hall. 'The bedrooms are upstairs.'

Lizzie followed Hannah upstairs. There were three doors. Hannah opened the one on the right.

'This is your room,' she said.

Lizzie was surprised. The room was really pretty. The walls were pale blue and it was much brighter[1] than the other rooms downstairs. There was a lovely blue cover on the bed too.

'Oh it's lovely!' said Lizzie.

Hannah looked at her and for a moment Lizzie saw a little light in those sad green eyes. Then it was gone again.

'Right!' continued Hannah. 'Here's the bathroom ... and that's my room,' she said pointing

---

[1] **brighter** more light

The Boy with the Red Balloon

to the closed door opposite Lizzie's room. 'Just one thing … please never go into my room … the rest of the house is yours, OK?'

'Sure, no problem,' said Lizzie. 'If you don't mind, I'd like to have a rest now. I didn't sleep much last night.'

'OK, I'll be downstairs or in the garden.'

Lizzie stayed in her room until dinner time. Hannah made some salad. They ate in silence¹. After dinner, Lizzie went into the living room. There was something missing … there was no television! *Fantastic!* thought Lizzie. All she could do was go to bed.

Hannah was already in her room. Lizzie could see a light was on from under the door. *Humph! She didn't even say goodnight!* thought Lizzie. *What a strange woman!* Lizzie went into her room and closed the door quietly. She didn't want any problems with horrible Hannah in the other room. *Let's hope tomorrow's better,* she thought.

> Hannah doesn't even have a television so all Lizzie can do is go to bed. Hannah doesn't even say goodnight to her. Lizzie hopes tomorrow will be better.

> *Think*
> Why do you think Hannah isn't very friendly?

---

¹ **in silence** (here) without speaking

After-reading Activities • Chapter 2

Reading A2 Key

1 **Read the sentences about Chapter 2. Choose the correct word (A, B or C).**

  Lizzie didn't eat ___much___ for breakfast the next morning.
  - **A** lots   **B** much   **C** many
1 They hope Hannah will look _____ Lizzie.
  - **A** after   **B** for   **C** at
2 Her parents _____ on the platform until the train disappeared.
  - **A** stood   **B** arrived   **C** went
3 Finally the train arrived _____ York.
  - **A** to   **B** in   **C** at
4 Lizzie felt a _____ afraid when she saw Hannah.
  - **A** few   **B** lot   **C** bit
5 It was going to be the _____ summer of Lizzie's life.
  - **A** bad   **B** worse   **C** worst

Grammar

2 **Choose the correct word(s).**

  It was cloudy when Lizzie *woke up* / *was waking up*.
1 Lizzie *was packing* / *packed* her bag when her mum came into her room.
2 Lizzie says she *won't* / *didn't* need any of her new summer stuff in the countryside.
3 Mrs Hammond *has spoken* / *spoke* to Hannah the day before.
4 Lizzie *wanted* / *was wanting* to have a rest before dinner.
5 Hannah *made* / *has made* salad for dinner that night.

Speaking

21st Century Skills

3 Discuss the following questions with a partner. Then tell the class what you agree and don't agree on.
1 Do you think Lizzie was right to be angry with her mum and dad? Why / Why not?
2 Would you like to spend your summer holidays in the countryside? Why? / Why not?
3 Do you think Lizzie will be happy in the countryside? Why? / Why not?
4 Do you like Hannah? Why? / Why not?

Before-reading Activity

Listening

▶ 6 **4** Listen to the start of Chapter 3 and choose the best word(s) to complete the sentences.

   Lizzie woke up *early* / *late* the next morning.
1 It was *cloudy* / *sunny*.
2 There was toast, butter and *jam* / *ham* for breakfast.
3 Lizzie pulled her phone out of her *pocket* / *bag*.
4 Her phone *was* / *wasn't* working.
5 Lizzie finished drinking her *tea* / *coffee*.
6 Hannah told her to go *for a walk* / *and work*.
7 The wood was *quiet and cool* / *quite old*.

Chapter 3

A Strange Meeting in the Woods

▶ 6   Lizzie woke up early next morning. It was a lovely sunny day. She got dressed and went downstairs for breakfast. Hannah was already in the kitchen.

'Good morning, Hannah,' she said.

'Your breakfast is ready, Elizabeth,' said Hannah.

'Oh! OK. If you want, you can call me Lizzie.'

Hannah didn't answer. They sat opposite each other at the table. There was toast, butter, and jam. *No sausages and bacon here,* thought Lizzie. She pulled her phone out of her pocket. *Maybe someone has sent me a message*, she thought.

'It won't work,' said Hannah.

'Sorry?' said Lizzie.

'Your phone … it won't work here in the countryside.'

'What! I don't believe it!' shouted Lizzie.

'Well, well,' said Hannah, 'and your mother said you were a nice quiet girl. Instead, look at you! All angry just because your phone doesn't work!'

Hannah makes a very simple breakfast the next morning. Then Lizzie becomes really angry when Hannah says that her phone won't work in the countryside.

❯ Lizzie is looking at her phone to see if she has any messages, but it isn't working.

Silvana Sardi

Lizzie decides to go for a walk in the woods. Suddenly she hears someone and sees a boy sitting on a branch with a red balloon tied next to him. ▶ 7

Lizzie said nothing. She stared[1] at her mobile and finished her toast and tea. *I need to get out of here,* she thought.

'What can I do now?' she asked Hannah.

'Go for a walk. Get some fresh air and forget about your phone,' said Hannah coldly[2].

Lizzie didn't answer. She stood up and went out leaving Hannah still sitting at the table.

She walked along a path and came to a wood. It was quiet and cool[3] there. She carried on walking. What else could she do? Finally, she sat down. There was a lake nearby[4]. ⬛

'Hey! Are you *Little Red Riding* Hood lost in the woods?' said someone.

'Who's there?' shouted Lizzie. She felt scared. She couldn't see anyone.

'I'm up here!'

She looked up. There was a boy sitting on the branch[5] of a big tree. Near him, tied[6] to the branch, was a red balloon.

➤ A boy is sitting on a branch of a tree with a red balloon tied next to him.

[1] **stare** look at for a long time
[2] **coldly** not in a friendly way
[3] **cool** (here) fresh
[4] **nearby** not far
[5] **branch** part of a tree
[6] **tied** see page 33. The balloon is tied to the tree

Silvana Sardi

At first Lizzie is scared, but the boy called Jack is friendly and he's also good-looking! Lizzie tells him that she's staying with a really strange woman.

'Who are you? What do you want?' asked Lizzie, still scared.

'Don't be afraid. I'm Jack. Are you new here?' Jack jumped down from the tree. Lizzie could see him better now. He was gorgeous[1]! He had brown hair and beautiful green eyes!

'Yes, no, I mean …' *Not again!* she thought. *Every time I meet a gorgeous guy, I forget how to speak!* She looked down. Her face was becoming redder and redder.

'Let's start again, eh?' said Jack laughing. 'I'm sorry if I scared you. My name's Jack, you know like in the story 'Jack and the Beanstalk'.'

Lizzie laughed. 'I'm Elizabeth, like *'Queen Elizabeth'* but my friends call me Lizzie.'

'So can I call you Lizzie?' asked Jack smiling.

'Yeah, why not. I really need a friend right now,' said Lizzie smiling too.

Jack sat down next to her. She told him where she was from and why she was there.

'Who are you staying with?' he asked.

'A really strange woman,' said Lizzie.

---

[1] **gorgeous** very good-looking

The Boy with the Red Balloon

'What's her name?' Jack asked.

'Hannah,' said Lizzie.

Jack looked at her surprised for a moment. 'And don't you like Hannah?' he asked.

'Well, she's very quiet and she doesn't have a TV and she's not very friendly,' said Lizzie quickly. *Oh no!* she thought. *Maybe he knows her… Why can't I keep my big mouth shut[1]?*

'Maybe you both need some more time together,' said Jack. 'I'm sure you'll like her in the end.'

'Maybe … and then I can't even use my phone here.' She pulled her phone out of her pocket to show Jack.

'Is that your phone?' he asked.

'Well what do you think it is? A pink elephant? What's the matter with it?' shouted Lizzie, angrily. 'I know it's not the latest model[2], but it's still a phone!'

Jack said nothing. He looked down at his feet. He wasn't smiling anymore. Lizzie felt sorry. *What am I doing?* she said to herself. *Here's this really*

> Jack is surpised that Lizzie doesn't like Hannah. Lizzie is worried now that maybe Jack knows Hannah.
>
> Lizzie gets angry with Jack when he asks if that's her phone, then she feels sorry again because he's upset.

---

[1] **shut** closed
[2] **model** type

Silvana Sardi

> Lizzie says she's sorry for shouting at Jack. They decide to go for a walk and they run up the hill together. It's fun even if it's not what Lizzie usually does with her friends and she feels happy.

nice guy, maybe somebody to talk to in this boring place ... and what do I do? ... Shout at him!

'Hey! I'm sorry,' she said. 'I was only joking[1]. Why don't we go for a walk?'

'Yeah, ok!' said Jack, happily. 'Come on, I'll show you a place with a great view ... but maybe a city girl like you can't climb hills' he said laughing. 'Come on, Lazy Lizzie! Let's see how fast you can run!'

Lizzie followed him, laughing and shouting. This wasn't what she usually did with her friends but it was fun. They ran out of the woods and up the hill. At the top, Lizzie threw herself onto the grass. Her face was bright red and her blue eyes were shining[2]. Jack lay on his side next to her. He looked down at her and smiled. For a second, their eyes met and Lizzie felt a thousand butterflies[3] dancing in her stomach.

'Your face is the same colour as your hair now!' said Jack laughing.

Lizzie sat there for a moment. *Well,* she thought, *one thing is sure, he doesn't fancy me. I probably look like a tomato!* But she felt happy.

---

[1] **joke** say something funny
[2] **shine** what the sun does
[3] **butterfly**

The Boy with the Red Balloon

'How old are you Lizzie?' Jack asked.

'Fourteen and three quarters. I'll be fifteen in November'.

'Well, my birthday's in August, on the 18th. So, if you're almost fifteen, then that means I'm almost seventeen!' said Jack laughing.

Jack says something strange: his birthday is on 18th August, and if Lizzie is almost 15 then he must be almost 17.

She thought that was a strange thing to say but she didn't have time to ask. Jack was already standing up and ready to go.

'Come on,' he said. 'There's still lots to see before you have to go home!'

Later that day, a happy Lizzie went back to the cottage. Hannah was drying the dishes in the kitchen.

'Hello, Hannah!' shouted Lizzie happily.

'Oh, you're back! Where have you been all this time?' said Hannah.

Back at the cottage, Hannah tells Lizzie she shouldn't talk to strangers.

'I went for a walk and I met this really nice boy,' said Lizzie.

'Which boy? Don't you know it's dangerous to speak to strangers[1]?' said Hannah. 'You should be more careful!'

'But he's nice. His name's Jack, and he's nearly

---

[1] **stranger** a person you don't know

seventeen. His birthday's in August, on the 18th and ...'

CRASH! The cup Hannah was holding suddenly fell to the ground. Her face was even whiter than usual.

'Hey! Are you OK? Come and sit down, before you fall down,' said Lizzie.

Hannah sat down slowly on the chair. She was staring at Lizzie in a strange way. Then she said:

'What's he like?'

'Oh, he's just gorgeous! He's got lovely brown wavy hair, and green eyes and a fantastic smile!' said Lizzie excitedly.

'Green eyes?' asked Hannah quietly.

'Yes, a bit like yours actually but brighter ...'

Hannah was staring at Lizzie again in that strange way.

'Oh sorry, I didn't mean to be rude[1],' said Lizzie. 'Your eyes are nice too!'

For the first time, Hannah smiled. 'Go and wash your hands, Lizzie. Dinner is ready,' she said.

Hannah drops a cup when Lizzie tells her about Jack and needs to sit down. Lizzie says Jack's eyes are green like Hannah's. Hannah smiles for the first time when she hears this.

---

[1] **rude** not polite

The Boy with the Red Balloon

They sat down at the kitchen table but this time they didn't eat in silence. Hannah wanted to know everything about Jack. She said she didn't know the boy. Maybe he was staying with someone in one of the farmhouses nearby. Lizzie couldn't believe it! Hannah was glad she had a friend! *Hannah isn't so bad after all,* thought Lizzie.

During the night, Lizzie woke up. She was thirsty. She wanted to go downstairs and get a glass of water. She opened her door quietly, then stopped. Hannah's bedroom door was open. The light was on. There was a big book open on the bed, maybe a photo album[1]. Lizzie couldn't see very well.

Suddenly, the bathroom door opened and Hannah was standing there in front of her.

'What are you doing?' said Hannah angrily. 'What are you looking at? Were you in my room?'

'No, no!' said Lizzie quickly. 'I just wanted a glass of water. I'm thirsty.'

'Well, go and get it!' said Hannah coldly.

Hannah wants to know all about Jack. She says she doesn't know him. Lizzie thinks maybe the woman isn't so bad after all.

During the night, Lizzie wants something to drink. Hannah's bedroom door is open. Hannah comes out of the bathroom and is angry because she thinks Lizzie was looking in her room, the one room in the house she told her not to go into.

---

[1] **photo album** a book where you put photos

Silvana Sardi

The next morning, Hannah is quiet like she was before and Lizzie says nothing about what happened during the night. After breakfast, she goes to the woods again.

'Goodnight!' She went back into her bedroom and closed the door behind her.

'Goodnight!' said Lizzie to the closed door.

The next morning, Hannah was very quiet. Lizzie didn't say anything about the night before. She ate her breakfast quickly and then left for the woods. ■

Think
Why do you think Hannah doesn't want Lizzie to go into her bedroom?

>
Hannah's bedroom door is open and Lizzie sees a book on her bed, maybe a photo album.

After-reading Activities • Chapter 3

Reading Comprehension

1 Put the sentences in the correct order as they happen in Chapter 3 of the story.

- **A** [1] Lizzie checked her phone for messages.
- **B** ☐ Lizzie met Jack.
- **C** ☐ Lizzie was thirsty during the night.
- **D** ☐ Lizzie and Jack climbed to the top of the hill.
- **E** ☐ Hannah told Lizzie to go for a walk.
- **F** ☐ Lizzie showed Jack her phone.
- **G** ☐ Lizzie told Hannah about Jack.
- **H** ☐ Lizzie sat down near a lake.

Grammar

2 Choose the best word to complete the sentences about the story.

Lizzie couldn't receive ~~any~~ / *no* messages on her phone.

1. It was sunny. There were *lots of* / *no* clouds in the blue sky.
2. Lizzie didn't say *something* / *anything* to Hannah when she left after breakfast.
3. Lizzie felt scared when she heard *everyone* / *someone* in the woods.
4. Jack said *nothing* / *anything* when Lizzie shouted at him about her phone.
5. Perhaps Jack was staying with *anyone* / *someone* nearby.
6. Hannah wanted to know *everything* / *everywhere* about Jack.
7. Hannah didn't say *a* / *any* word the next morning.

Writing A2 Key

3 You're Lizzie. Write to your friend, Rachel:

– Ask her about her summer in Blackpool.
– Tell her about Hannah.
– Tell her about Jack.

Write between 25 and 35 words.

Speaking and Writing

21st Century Skills

4 In Chapter 3, Lizzie is angry because her phone doesn't work in the countryside. Discuss these questions with a partner and write your answers.

1. What do you use your phone for?
2. How much time do you spend on your phone?
3. Do you prefer doing lessons online or in the classroom? Why?
4. Do you prefer watching television or something on your PC? Why?
5. When do you use computers at school?
6. Do you use social networking sites? Why? / Why not?

Before-reading Activity

Speaking

5 Discuss these questions with a partner. Now read Chapter 4 to see if you were right.

1. Will Lizzie bring Jack to the cottage to meet Hannah?
2. Will Lizzie's parents come to visit her?
3. Will Jack and Lizzie go shopping in York?
4. Will Lizzie and Hannah become good friends?

Chapter 4

Summer Love

> 8 Lizzie and Jack met every day. He was always there waiting for her, sitting in the tree near the lake with the red balloon tied to the branch.

'What's the balloon for?' asked Lizzie one day.
'It's there to help me remember,' said Jack.
'Remember what?'
'Where I have to meet a pretty girl with red hair!' he said laughing.

Soon Lizzie began to forget about Blackpool, her friends and even Greg! She and Jack talked for hours. Jack loved the woods and told her funny stories about all the animals that lived there. They were quite childlike[1] but she loved them. He was different from all the other boys she knew. He wanted to know everything about her. Most boys only wanted to talk about cars and football or themselves! She even told him about Greg.

'Greg is probably with Jenny now,' said Lizzie.
'Who's Jenny?' asked Jack.
'Oh, just the most beautiful girl in the school.'

Lizzie and Jack meet every day and soon Lizzie starts to forget about Blackpool, her friends and even Greg. Jack tells her a lot of funny, childlike stories and she loves them. He's not like other boys who always talk about themselves. He wants to know about her.

---

[1] **childlike** innocent - refers to the positive qualities of a child

The Boy with the Red Balloon

'Hey! And what's wrong with you? You're the prettiest girl I've ever met, Lizzie ... and you're fun, too. If Greg prefers Jenny, then he's crazy!'

Lizzie looked at him. She felt very strange inside. Was this love?

They were lying on the grass near 'their' tree with the red balloon. It was very hot that day.

'Let's go for a swim in the lake,' said Lizzie.

'No!' shouted Jack. He was really angry.

Lizzie was surprised. 'Ok! Don't shout!'

Jack was quiet for a moment, then he said:

'Hey, Lizzie, I'm sorry. I didn't mean to shout. But, please, never go into the lake. It's really dangerous. Please say you won't.'

'OK, OK, I won't!' she said angrily.

She lay back down on the grass and closed her eyes. There was a strange silence between them.

'Friends again?' asked Jack quietly.

Lizzie opened her eyes. His face was very near hers. *Is he going to kiss me?* she thought.

She closed her eyes again. Then Jack kissed her ... but on the nose!

Oh well, better than nothing, she thought.

> When Jack says Lizzie is really pretty, she feels strange inside. Maybe it's love.

> Jack gets really angry with Lizzie when she has the idea of swimming in the lake. He says it's very dangerous. Then Jack says he's sorry for shouting at her and Lizzie thinks that he's going to kiss her!

Silvana Sardi

That evening, she told Hannah about her day.

'I don't know why Jack got so angry about the lake,' said Lizzie.

'Maybe nobody taught him to swim,' said Hannah quietly.

'Of course!' said Lizzie. 'I didn't think of that! You understand him better than I do!'

'I'm older than you,' said Hannah. 'I've made more mistakes than you … sooner or later, you learn from your mistakes.'

'Mum taught me to swim when I was very young,' said Lizzie.

'Yes,' said Hannah quietly. 'Your mum did the right thing. You're a lucky girl, Lizzie.' There were tears in her eyes. *Oh no! I've upset[1] her!* thought Lizzie.

'Are you OK, Hannah?' she asked.

'Yes, don't worry … it's nothing … but remember, Lizzie, never swim in the lake, it's really dangerous.'

'Yeah, I know, I know. You're as bad as Jack!' said Lizzie laughing.

Hannah says maybe Jack was angry about the lake because he can't swim. She says Lizzie's mum did the right thing teaching her to swim and she starts to cry. She also tells Lizzie never to swim in the lake.

Lizzie is lying on the grass with her eyes closed. Jack has just asked her to be friends again and she thinks he's going to kiss her.

[1] **upset** when you make someone feel sad

Silvana Sardi

Jack says he made a big mistake once that made a lot of people sad, especially one person. Lizzie tells him that Hannah talked about making mistakes and learning from them. Jack says 'sooner or later' the same words Hannah used.

One afternoon, Lizzie took a book with her. It was a fantasy-horror story. Jack looked at the front cover. There was a scary face on it.

'Why are you reading that?' he asked. 'I only like stories with a happy ending.'

'Yeah, OK,' said Lizzie, 'but sometimes in life there isn't a happy ending.'

'I know,' he said. He looked away, his face sad.

'Hey, are you OK, Jack?' asked Lizzie, worried.

He looked at her and smiled, but it wasn't his usual big, happy smile.

'Yeah, I'm fine ... just remembering the time I made a big mistake. I made a lot of people sad ... especially one.'

'We all make mistakes, Jack. It's strange ... the other day Hannah was talking about mistakes. She said that we all learn from our mistakes.'

'Sooner or later,' said Jack quietly.

'That's what Hannah said too! I'm sure you didn't want to hurt anyone, Jack. You're the kindest guy I know!'

'And how many guys do you know, city girl?'

The Boy with the Red Balloon

'Lots and lots and lots!' said Lizzie, laughing. She was glad to see Jack was happy again.

That day, he made daisy chains[1] for her. Then he put them on her head and around her neck.

'Lovely Lizzie, Queen of the Woods!' he sang.

She really felt like a queen with Jack. As evening arrived, he said: 'Come on, Lazy Lizzie, it's time to go home. Mum will be worried.'

'What? You mean your mum still worries about you? But you're almost seventeen!' said Lizzie.

'Oh! You know mums … I'll always be her little boy,' said Jack.

He smiled, but it was a sad smile. Lizzie noticed[2] but said nothing. He never talked about his family. Maybe he had problems at home. She didn't want to ask so she smiled and said:

'Yes, you're right. My parents still think I'm their little girl. They always want to know where I'm going, who I'm with, when I'm coming home …'

'It's because they love you, Lizzie, always remember that,' said Jack quietly.

Jack tells Lizzie it's time to go home because Mum will be worried. Lizzie is surprised that his mum still worries about him now that he's almost 17. Smiling sadly, Jack says he'll always be his mum's little boy. Lizzie thinks that maybe he has problems at home.

---

[1] **daisy chains** necklaces made of little white flowers
[2] **notice** see

Silvana Sardi

Jack tells Lizzie to always remember that her parents love her and kisses her on her nose again! No real kiss yet.

He walked her to the edge¹ of the woods.

'Bye, Lizzie, see you tomorrow!' he said kissing her on the nose. Again! thought Lizzie. She was still waiting for her first 'real' kiss!

'Bye, Jack! See you!'

When she got back to the cottage, Hannah was in the garden.

'Hi, Lizzie! Just in time!' said Hannah. I've made a picnic for us. It's a lovely warm evening.'

'Wow!' said Lizzie. 'You've made so much stuff!'

When Lizzie arrives back at the cottage, she notices that Hannah looks younger and happier. Her clothes and hair are much prettier. Hannah says that Lizzie has made her happy again.

They sat down to eat. Hannah was different today: younger-looking, and happier too. She was wearing a yellow T-shirt and a bright skirt with flowers. Her soft blonde hair fell around her face.

'I like your new clothes,' said Lizzie. 'And your hair too! You look² so young and happy!'

Hannah smiled. 'Thanks, Lizzie,' she said. 'You've made me happy again!'

> **Hannah has made a picnic in the garden. She looks younger and happier than before.**

Think
Do you like having picnics? Why? / Why not?

¹ **edge** where something starts or finishes
² **look** give the idea that

After-reading Activities • **Chapter 4**

Reading A2 Key

1 Complete the sentences about Chapter 4 with the correct answer (A, B or C).

Lizzie and Jack meet ___every___ day.
- **A** all
- **B** many
- **C** every ✓

1 Jack _____ Lizzie funny stories about all the animals in the woods.
- **A** says
- **B** tells
- **C** speaks

2 Jack wants to know _____ about Lizzie.
- **A** everything
- **B** nothing
- **C** everywhere

3 Lizzie wants to go _____ a swim in the lake.
- **A** to
- **B** at
- **C** for

4 Jack says the lake is _____ dangerous for swimming.
- **A** enough
- **B** much
- **C** too

5 Lizzie says her mum _____ her to swim.
- **A** learnt
- **B** taught
- **C** made

6 Jack says he _____ a big mistake in the past.
- **A** made
- **B** did
- **C** had

Speaking and Writing

2 Talk to a partner about the following questions, then write your ideas.

1 How has Lizzie changed since the start of the story?
2 What do you know about Jack?
3 How has Hannah changed?

21st Century Skills

Grammar

3 **Complete the sentences with the comparative or superlative of the words in the box.**

> ~~interesting~~ funny beautiful pretty
> hot good kind

Lizzie thinks Jack is ___more interesting___ than other boys she knows.
1 Lizzie thinks Hannah understands Jack _____ than she does.
2 Jack says Lizzie is the _____ girl he has ever met.
3 Jack's stories are the _____ Lizzie has ever heard.
4 Lizzie thinks Jenny is _____ than she is.
5 That day was much _____ than any other day.
6 Lizzie says Jack is the _____ guy she knows.

Before-reading Activity

Listening

4 **Listen to the start of Chapter 5. Decide if the sentences are true (T) or false (F).**

	T	F
Lizzie woke up at her usual time.	☐	✓
1 She had breakfast after getting dressed.	☐	☐
2 Hannah was in the garden.	☐	☐
3 There was a big breakfast waiting for Lizzie.	☐	☐
4 Lizzie ate slowly.	☐	☐
5 Lizzie ran to the woods.	☐	☐
6 Jack wasn't waiting at their usual place.	☐	☐

Chapter 5

The Lake

Lizzie runs all the way to the woods but Jack isn't there.

▶ 9   Lizzie woke up late next morning. She got dressed quickly and ran downstairs. Hannah was in the kitchen.

'Good morning, Lizzie! Did you sleep well?'

'Hi, Hannah! Yes thanks … but it's really late!'

'Don't worry, I'm sure Jack will wait for you,' said Hannah smiling. 'Come and have some breakfast. I've made you sausage, bacon and eggs.'

'Mmm! Yummy!' said Lizzie.

She wanted to leave immediately, but she didn't want to be rude. She sat down and ate as quickly as possible.

'That was lovely, Hannah, thanks!' she said, pushing the last sausage into her mouth. 'See you later!'

'Have fun!' said Hannah as Lizzie ran out the door.

Lizzie ran all the way to the woods. She arrived at their usual meeting place. Jack wasn't there! *That's strange*, she thought. ■

▶ 10   She sat down on the grass to wait. It was very hot now. She looked up at the tree. The red

Jack's red balloon is in the middle of the lake. When Lizzie sees it she's afraid because she remembers Hannah saying that maybe Jack doesn't know how to swim.

Silvana Sardi

balloon wasn't there! She felt worried … she didn't know why. She looked around.

Suddenly she saw the balloon. It was in the middle of the lake! She jumped up.

'Jack! Jack!' she shouted.

She remembered Hannah's words: *'Maybe nobody taught him to swim …'*

Lizzie jumped into the lake without thinking. She didn't even take off her trainers. The water was cold … very cold. She started swimming towards the balloon. Then she felt something around her feet … water reeds[1]! They were pulling her under! She tried to keep her head above the water, but the reeds were around her legs now, pulling her down … down to the bottom of the lake. The water was over her head now. She closed her eyes …

Suddenly, Jack was there. He had his arms around her. He was pulling her up and out of the water. He kissed her … this time on the lips[2], and she felt warm inside again.

'Hey! Lazy Lizzie, wake up!' said Jack. 'Your face is all red with the sun!'

When Lizzie sees the balloon in the lake she immediately jumps in because she thinks Jack is under the water. The water is cold and the water reeds start to pull her under. Then suddenly Jack pulls her out of the water and kisses her on the lips.

---

[1] **water reeds** a plant that grows under water
[2] **lips** mouth

The Boy with the Red Balloon

Lizzie opened her eyes. Jack was smiling at her. She didn't understand ... she felt her face. He was right; it was hot. She felt her clothes ... they were dry. She looked up; the balloon was tied to its usual branch.

'But the balloon ... the lake ... you!' she said. She started to cry.

'Hey Lizzie, don't cry, you've had a bad dream, that's all. Don't worry, I'm here now.'

Jack held her in his arms until she was calm[1] again.

'Oh, Jack, it was terrible,' she said. 'I was in the lake and I was drowning[2] but you saved[3] me.' She didn't tell him about the kiss, the real kiss.

'Well, it was definitely a dream!' said Jack smiling. 'I can't swim!'

So, Hannah was right, thought Lizzie. She felt a bit stupid[4] now so she laughed and said:

'Well, the next time I have a problem in water, I won't call you!'

'You'll always be safe with me, Lizzie. I'm your 'Prince' and you're my 'Sleeping Beauty!'

Lizzie wakes up. Her face is red with the sun and her clothes are dry. The balloon is tied to the tree as usual. Jack says it was a bad dream. When Lizzie tells him how he saved her, Jack laughs and says it was was definitely a dream because he can't swim. Lizzie remembers Hannah's words.

---

[1] **calm** quiet
[2] **drown** die under water
[3] **save** help someone in danger
[4] **stupid** not clever

Silvana Sardi

Jack and Lizzie have a great day together and Lizzie is in love with him. Back at the cottage, Hannah quickly closes the book she's looking at and Lizzie knows for sure it's the photo album that she saw before on Hannah's bed.

said Jack. 'Come on! Let's get some fresh air at the top of the hill. It's too hot here today.'

'You and your fairy tales[1] Jack! You're just a big baby!' said Lizzie, smiling.

This time they didn't run up the hill like the first day, but walked hand in hand. Lizzie felt safe.

They played at being Prince and Princess. Prince Jack made Princess Lizzie a bed of flowers. He sang her songs and picked berries[2] for her to eat. They had a lovely afternoon together. Lizzie was in love. Her first summer love and it felt great!

When she got back to the cottage, Hannah was in the garden with a big book. She closed it quickly when she saw Lizzie.

'Hi, Lizzie, back already?' she said. 'I'll just put this upstairs and then I'll get dinner ready.'

That was the book I saw that night, thought Lizzie. It was a photo album. She was sure now. It was clear that Hannah didn't want her to see it, so she said nothing.

Hannah made fish and chips that night and Lizzie told her about her day with Jack and her dream.

---

[1] **fairy tales** stories of magic for children
[2] **berry** a small kind of fruit

The Boy with the Red Balloon

Hannah listened carefully.

'So in your dream he wasn't afraid of water,' she said quietly. Then, she smiled, stood up and kissed Lizzie on the nose. 'You're a great girl, Lizzie, always remember that!'

Lizzie was so surprised she didn't know what to say. *This nose kissing must be something they do in Yorkshire,* she thought.

She smiled at Hannah. She was really pretty that evening. She looked so young, so happy, not like when Lizzie first arrived.

'Oh, I forgot to tell you,' said Hannah. 'Your mum phoned this afternoon. The roof is almost finished, so they're coming to get you tomorrow.'

'But I don't want to go home!' shouted Lizzie. 'I love it here! I want to stay with you and Jack!'

'Oh Lizzie! How you've changed. You were so angry when you arrived. Do you remember?' said Hannah.

'Yes,' said Lizzie, 'but it's different now …'

'I know,' said Hannah. 'You've made things different. Your love has made things different here.'

Hannah is happy that Jack wasn't afraid of water in Lizzie's dream. Instead, Lizzie isn't happy when she hears that her parents are coming to get her the next day. She's very different from when she first came and hated the countryside.

Silvana Sardi

Tomorrow is Jack's birthday and Lizzie wants to buy him a present. Hannah says she'll take her.

'Oh, Hannah! But tomorrow's special. I can't go home tomorrow. It's the 18th of August, Jack's birthday!'

'I know,' said Hannah quietly.

'How do you know?' said Lizzie surprised.

'You told me, don't you remember?' said Hannah.

'Oh, of course! I forgot. So can we go into town and get him a present?'

Hannah smiled. 'Don't worry Lizzie, we can go together tomorrow. Now, off to bed, you've had a long day.'

When Lizzie gets ready for bed, she notices some water reeds in her clothes and this makes her feel cold inside.

Lizzie went upstairs. She got undressed. She threw her clothes on the floor, put on her nightdress[1] and sat on the bed. Suddenly she noticed something strange ... she felt cold inside ... there were some water reeds in her clothes on the floor!

> **Lizzie notices that there are some water reeds in her clothes on the floor - the ones she was wearing when she dreamt she was drowning that day.**

Think
What do you think Lizzie will buy Jack for his birthday?

[1] **nightdress** what you wear in bed

After-reading Activities • Chapter 5

Speaking and Writing

1 Discuss these questions about Chapter 5 with a partner and write your answers.

1 Why did Lizzie not really want to have breakfast?
2 Why did she feel worried when she got to their meeting place?
3 Why did she jump into the lake with all her clothes on?
4 Do you believe it was a dream? Why? / Why not?
5 How often do you dream and what do you usually dream about?

Reading A2 Key

2 Complete the sentences about Chapter 5 with the correct answer (A, B or C).

Hannah tells Lizzie that Jack will wait ____for____ her.
   A to   **B** at   **C** for

1 Lizzie felt the water reeds _____ her feet.
   A under   **B** around   **C** behind
2 Jack kissed Lizzie _____ the lips.
   A to   **B** at   **C** on
3 Jack is sure Lizzie only had a _____ dream.
   A bad   **B** worse   **C** worst
4 Jack tells Lizzie that she'll always be safe with _____ .
   A them   **B** him   **C** her
5 Hannah didn't want Lizzie _____ the photo album.
   A seeing   **B** see   **C** to see
6 Hannah is pleased that Jack wasn't afraid _____ water in Lizzie's dream.
   A of   **B** from   **C** to

Vocabulary

3 A **Unscramble these words from Chapter 5.**

tchknie ___kitchen___

1 woflser _____
2 lofor _____
3 mras _____
4 ntrisare _____
5 shpic _____
6 retnanfoo _____

3 B **Now use each word once to complete the sentences below.**

Hannah was in the ___kitchen___ when Lizzie came downstairs.

1 Lizzie didn't take off her _____ before jumping into the lake.
2 Jack held Lizzie in his _____ until she stopped crying.
3 Jack made Lizzie a bed of _____ .
4 They had a lovely _____ together.
5 Hannah made fish and _____ for dinner that night.
6 That night, Lizzie threw her clothes on the _____ .

Before-reading Activity

Listening

11 4 Listen and make true sentences about Chapter 6.

1 Lizzie woke up when the *phone / alarm clock* rang.
2 *Hannah / Lizzie* answered the phone.
3 Lizzie says everything is *great / horrible* in the countryside.
4 Lizzie's mum was *surprised / happy* when she heard the name 'Jack'.
5 Her mum tells her the roof *is / isn't* finished.

Chapter 6

Past Meeting Present

▶ 11 The phone was ringing downstairs. Lizzie woke up. *Hannah will get it*, thought Lizzie. She turned over and tried to go back to sleep. The phone kept ringing.

'OK! I'm coming! I'm coming!' said Lizzie.
She ran downstairs to the phone.
'Hello!'
'Hello! Lizzie? It's Mum!'
'Oh, hello Mum!'
'Well, how are you Lizzie?'
'Fine! Everything is great here!'
'Really?' said her mum. 'That's a surprise!'

'Yeah, I know!' said Lizzie, laughing. 'Listen, Mum, I'm really sorry about how I acted when I left. I was really horrible to you and Dad. I was only thinking about myself.'

'Don't worry, Lizzie. Your dad and I were sorry too. We didn't want to spoil[1] your summer.'

> Lizzie wakes up to the phone ringing. It's her mum and she's surprised to hear that Lizzie is happy in the countryside.

---

[1] **spoil** make something bad

The Boy with the Red Balloon

'But you haven't!' said Lizzie. 'I love it here!'

'Oh, that's good. We were worried that the country was going to be boring for you.'

'No, not at all!' said Lizzie. 'I've met a boy, Mum. He's gorgeous.'

'Aha! Now I understand,' said her mum, laughing. 'So what's this gorgeous guy's name?'

'Jack.' said Lizzie.

'JACK?' said her mum surprised.

'Yes, you know, like *Jack and the Beanstalk*.'

Lizzie laughed, remembering the first day she met Jack.

'That's strange,' her mum said quietly.

'What's strange about it? It's a name like any other name,' said Lizzie angrily.

'OK, calm down, Lizzie. I'm sure he's a nice boy. I'm glad you've had somebody to talk to. But did Hannah tell you the good news? The roof is finished! You can come home!'

12 'Yeah, she told me,' said Lizzie quietly.

'What's wrong? Don't you want to come home?'

'Yes, of course, Mum,' said Lizzie. 'It's just … it's

Lizzie tells her mum that she's met a boy called Jack. Her mum becomes quiet when she hears that name and says it's strange. She tells Lizzie that the roof is finished so she can come home but she can hear that Lizzie isn't happy about the idea.

Silvana Sardi

Lizzie's mum shouts on the phone when she hears that today, 18th August, is Jack's birthday. She's in the car on her way to the cottage with Lizzie's dad. She wants to speak to Hannah.

Lizzie is angry that her mum is so strange on the phone. She looks for Hannah but can't find her in the kitchen and there's no breakfast on the table.

just … oh, Mum, it's Jack's birthday today and I want to get him a present …'

'JACK'S BIRTHDAY!' shouted her mum.

'Yeah, the 18th of August is his birthday. What's so strange about that?' said Lizzie.

There was silence on the other end of the phone.

'Mum? Are you still there?'

'Yes … yes, Lizzie,' said her mum. 'Listen, I'm in the car with your dad. We'll be there soon. But go and get Hannah, I need to speak to her.'

'In the car? Already? But, I don't …'

'Lizzie! Do as I say! Go and get Hannah!' shouted her mum.

'OK! OK! I'll go and get her,' said Lizzie angrily.

She took the phone with her. 'Hannah! Hannah! Where are you? Mum's on the phone!' she shouted.

No answer.

Lizzie went into the kitchen. There was no one there. There was no breakfast on the table. *Maybe she's out in the garden,* she thought. She opened the front door and went out to the garden.

The Boy with the Red Balloon

'Hannah!' Hannah!' she called.

No answer.

'Mum, I can't find her. Maybe she's gone to the shops or something,' said Lizzie.

'What about upstairs? See if she's in her room,' said her mum. 'Maybe she's still asleep.'

'Impossible, she always gets up really early.'

'Well, maybe she's having a shower.'

'OK! I'll go up and look,' said Lizzie.

Lizzie went upstairs. She listened at the bathroom door. She couldn't hear anything. She opened it … there was no one there.

'She's not in the bathroom, Mum,' said Lizzie.

'Well, try her room.'

'No! I can't! She doesn't want me to go into her room,' said Lizzie.

'Look, Lizzie!' said her mum. She was beginning to get really angry now. 'Knock[1] on the door!'

Lizzie stood in front of the door. She didn't want to go in. She felt she was doing something wrong … she felt afraid.

She knocked on the door softly and called:

> Hannah isn't in the garden or the bathroom. Lizzie doesn't want to look in Hannah's room but her mum starts to get really angry on the phone so Lizzie knocks on Hannah's bedroom door.

[1] **knock** hit with your hand

Silvana Sardi

Lizzie finds Hannah lying in bed with her eyes closed and the photo album next to her. Her face is pale but she looks beautiful. There's a newspaper article on the open page of the photo album.

'Hannah? Are you in there? Sorry to bother you, but Mum wants you on the phone.'

She waited ... no answer.

'Well?' said her mum.

'No answer,' said Lizzie.

'Well, open the door!' said Mrs Hammond angrily.

Lizzie stood looking at the door for a few seconds then slowly opened it. She could see Hannah lying on the bed. She walked over to her. On the bed was the photo album. It was open.

'Hannah?' she said.

No answer.

Hannah's eyes were closed. She was beautiful. Her face was pale but young looking. Her lovely blonde hair fell softly around her face. Lizzie didn't want to wake her up.

She looked at the photo album. There was an old newspaper article[1] on the open page. She read the title:

'Little boy drowns in lake'

Under the title there was a picture and an article.

Hannah is lying in bed. Her eyes are closed and the photo album is open next to her.

[1] **article** story

Silvana Sardi

Lizzie knows the two people in the picture in the newspaper. They're Hannah and Jack when they were both much younger.

Lizzie looked closer. There was a young, blonde woman with a little dark-haired boy in her arms. He was holding a red balloon. They both had the same bright green eyes. Lizzie knew those eyes ... a young Hannah and a very young Jack were smiling at her in the picture!

The article started like this:

18th August, terrible accident at lake. 3-year-old, Jack Jones drowns in the lake on his birthday while trying to get his red balloon. The little boy was with his mother, Hannah, for a birthday picnic in the woods. While his mum was busy putting the food out, the wind blew[1] the balloon into the middle of the lake. Jack tried to get it ... but he couldn't swim. It all happened so quickly. There was nothing his poor mother could do ...

The article tells the story of how Jack drowned in the lake on his birthday when he was only 3 years old. Hannah, his mother, could do nothing to save him. Lizzie tries to wake Hannah up but she's dead.

'Hannah! Hannah!' shouted Lizzie, shaking[2] her hard.

No answer. Hannah was cold, very cold.

'Nooooo! Nooooo!' shouted Lizzie.

'LIZZIE! LIZZIE!' her mum shouted on the other end of the phone.

---

[1] **blow** what the wind does
[2] **shake** move quickly

The Boy with the Red Balloon

The phone fell to the ground …
No answer.

• • •

It was early afternoon. Lizzie was sitting in the kitchen with her dad. Her mum was upstairs with the doctor. They heard the bedroom door open. Her mum came downstairs with the doctor. She was crying.

'I'm terribly sorry,' said the doctor, 'but there was nothing I could do. It was a heart attack[1]. Probably early this morning.'

'No!' cried Lizzie's mum. 'She died of a broken heart!'

Lizzie ran to her mum.

'Oh, Mum! Oh, Mum! Don't cry! I understand now. She isn't broken-hearted anymore. She's with Jack now. They're together at last. I'm going to miss them both so much, but I'm glad they're together again.'

Sara Hammond looked at her daughter.

'Oh Lizzie! You've changed so much,' she said. 'You're the best girl ever!'

> The doctor says that Hannah died of a heart attack. Lizzie will miss both her and Jack but she's glad they're together again at last.

> **Think**
> Why do you think Lizzie's mum is happy that her daughter has changed so much?

[1] **heart attack** when your heart stops

After-reading Activities • Chapter 6

Reading A2 Key

1. Complete the text about Chapter 6 with one word in each space.

Lizzie wakes ___up___ when her mum phones. Lizzie isn't happy at (**1**) _____ thought of going back home and she tells her mum about Jack. Her mum is surprised (**2**) _____ she hears the name Jack and gets even more worried when Lizzie says it's Jack's birthday that day, 18th August. She tells Lizzie she wants to speak to Hannah but Lizzie can't find (**3**) _____ anywhere. Lizzie's mum gets angrier on the phone and tells Lizzie (**4**) _____ go into Hannah's bedroom. Lizzie finds Hannah lying on the bed with her eyes closed and the photo album (**5**) _____ to her. The newspaper article tells the story of how Jack drowned in the lake (**6**) _____ his birthday when he was only three years old and his mother, Hannah, could do nothing to save him.

Speaking and Writing

21st Century Skills

2. Was the end of the story a surprise? Would you like to change it? Talk to your partner and write your ideas.

_____
_____
_____
_____
_____
_____
_____
_____
_____

Vocabulary

❸ How many new words can you make from the title: 'The Boy with the Red Balloon'? Read the clues and complete the table below.

1 The colour of the sun. (adj)
2 Not short. (adj)
3 You do this with a book. (v)
4 You do this with a pen. (v)
5 Jack sat in this. (n)
6 It comes after nine. (n)
7 You open this to go into a room. (n)
8 Lizzie and Jack always met here. (n)
9 The opposite of cold. (adj)
10 You do this with your ear. (v)
11 Jack often _____ Lizzie stories. (v – past simple)
12 Lizzie took this to travel to Yorkshire. (n)
13 The opposite of old. (adj)
14 The opposite of black. (adj)
15 Lizzie _____ lots of things about the countryside that she didn't know before. (v – past simple)

Verbs	Nouns	Adjectives
1	1	1
2	2	2
3	3	3
4	4	4
5	5	5

Focus on...

Blackpool

At the start of the story, Lizzie is really angry with her parents because she wants to stay in Blackpool with her friends for the summer. What's so special about Blackpool? Let's see!

Where is it?

Blackpool is a seaside town in Lancashire on the northwest coast of England. People started going on holiday there in the 18th century because it has beautiful, long sandy beaches. Millions of visitors still go to Blackpool every year to enjoy all the fun things it has to offer. Let's look at some of them.

Blackpool Tower

This Tower opened in 1984. It looks a bit like the Eiffel Tower in Paris. It's 158m high and at the top of the tower there's a glass Skywalk. If you're brave enough to walk on it, you can get great views of Blackpool, the Irish Sea and the north west of England. On your way to the top, you can also stop at the fantastic 4D cinema that tells the history of this special tower. There's also a circus and a famous ballroom, where they hold dance competitions.

Blackpool Promenade

Blackpool Promenade is the road that goes along the beach and there are lots of things to see and do in this part of the town. You can see trams, horses and carriages and, of course, you have to try the famous 'candy floss' or 'Blackpool Rock', both very sweet but very yummy too! Some people even get married on the Promenade!

Blackpool Illuminations

This fantastic lights show lasts sixty-six days and goes along 10 km of the promenade. It uses more than a million lights and each year they follow a different theme. The start of the festival, when they turn on the lights, is one of the biggest parties in Blackpool with free food and drink and fireworks too. One of the best ways to see the lights is to take a ride on a tram that goes slowly up and down the promenade.

Stanley Park

Stanley Park is full of beautiful flowers and green areas where you can sit and relax and have a picnic. There are also lots of things to do. You can take a pedalo or a boat and go for a ride on the lake. You can play tennis, basketball or football. If you prefer something different, you can try the BMX tracks, the skateboard park and trampolines. There's also a bandstand where bands play music in the summer and a little train that takes you around the park if you're too tired to walk.

Task - Internet

Look online for some more information about Blackpool, then plan a trip there with your friends. Decide:
- When to go, how long to stay, and what you'll see and do there.

Focus on...

Strange Stories

Do you like scary stories? There are lots of books and films about ghosts, magic and mystery. Let's look at some of them.

The Turn of the Screw

In the Victorian period, people loved ghost stories. One of the most famous is *The Turn of the Screw* by Henry James. He wrote this ghost story in 1898. It's about a woman who goes to work in a house in the country in England. She has to look after two children, Miles and Flora. Soon after she arrives, she starts to see two strange figures in the park around the house. Maybe they're the ghosts of two people who worked at the house but who are now both dead. She thinks that the children can see the ghosts and tries to help Miles and Flora. This story is very strange because Henry James doesn't tell the reader why the boy dies at the end, which makes it even scarier.

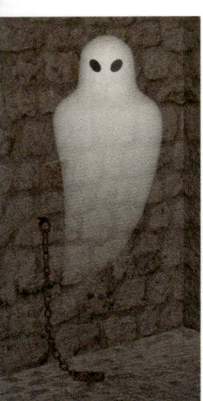

The Canterville Ghost

Not all stories about ghosts are scary. Some of them are even funny like *The Canterville Ghost* by Oscar Wilde. Wilde wrote this short story in 1887 and it's very different from other ghost stories. In the story, an American family goes to live in a big house in the English countryside, where there's a ghost called Sir Simon. The strange thing about this story is that the people aren't scared of the ghost, but Sir Simon is scared of the family, especially when the children make a 'fake'[1] ghost to frighten him.

[1] **fake** not real

Big Screen Ghosts

There are many films about ghosts and they're usually horror films or films about magic. Do you like them? Have you seen any of these on the next page?

The Others

This film was made in 2005. A woman, played by actress Nicole Kidman, lives in a dark, old house in the country with her two children. The children can't go outside because the sun is bad for them. Their mother tries to keep them as safe as possible. The woman soon begins to think the house is haunted[1] after her daughter draws a picture of four people she says she has seen in a room. They hear a lot of strange noises in the house, too and one day the mother discovers that the three people who were helping her to look after the house are actually all dead! The ending is even more surprising ... Why don't you watch it and see?

Harry Potter Films

The Harry Potter films are all about magic and there are lots of ghosts in them, too. In fact, lots of ghosts live in Hogwarts Castle and Sir Nicholas, (Nearly Headless Nick) a ghost himself, often helps Harry Potter. Sir Nicholas believes that ghosts were once wizards or witches so they were people who had special magical powers when they were alive. Hogwarts Castle has different houses and each house has its own ghost. There are more than twenty ghosts altogether. Sir Nicholas is in all the Harry Potter books but only in the first two films.

Task
Write about a film you have seen recently and say why you enjoyed it.

_____
_____
_____
_____
_____
_____

[1] **haunted** with ghosts

Test Yourself

How much can you remember? Choose A, B or C to complete the sentences about the story.

At the beginning of the story, Lizzie is
- **A** sad.
- **B** happy. ✓
- **C** angry.

1. Lizzie wants to spend the summer
   - **A** with her friends.
   - **B** with her mum and dad.
   - **C** in the countryside.

2. Lizzie travels from Blackpool to Yorkshire
   - **A** by car.
   - **B** by bus.
   - **C** by train.

3. Hannah's cottage
   - **A** has no garden.
   - **B** has only one floor.
   - **C** is a long way from the town.

4. On her first morning at the cottage, Lizzie discovers that
   - **A** she has left her phone at home.
   - **B** her phone doesn't work.
   - **C** Hannah has her phone.

5. When Lizzie meets Jack for the first time,
   - **A** he's sitting in a tree.
   - **B** he's lying on the grass.
   - **C** he's standing on a hill.

6. Jack tells Lizzie that his birthday is
   - **A** in August.
   - **B** in September.
   - **C** in November.

7. Lizzie wakes up during the night because
   - **A** she hears Hannah crying.
   - **B** she's thirsty.
   - **C** it's stormy outside.

8. Jack gets angry with Lizzie because
   - **A** she wants to swim in the lake.
   - **B** she doesn't like his stories.
   - **C** she doesn't like Hannah.

9. When Lizzie sees the red balloon in the lake
   - **A** she laughs.
   - **B** she climbs the tree.
   - **C** she jumps into the lake.

10. At the end of the story, Lizzie
    - **A** is angry with her parents.
    - **B** will miss Jack and Hannah.
    - **C** still hates the countryside.

Syllabus

Topics
Family
Friendship
Emotions
Mystery

Verbs
Positive and negative imperative forms
Present simple and present continuous (also for future reference)
Past simple and past continuous
Present perfect simple
Future with *going to* and *will*
Can, could, have to, need, would like, should for advice, *may* for possibility
Want someone to do something
Common phrasal verbs
Passive forms – present and past simple

Adjectives
Comparative and superlative forms

Adverbs
Regular and irregular forms

Teen ELi Readers

Stage 1
Maureen Simpson, *In Search of a Missing Friend*
Charles Dickens, *Oliver Twist*
Geoffrey Chaucer, *The Canterbury Tales*
Janet Borsbey & Ruth Swan, *The Boat Race Mystery*
Lucy Maud Montgomery, *Anne of Green Gables*
Mark Twain, *A Connecticut Yankee in King Arthur's Court*
Mark Twain, *The Adventures of Huckleberry Finn*
Angela Tomkinson, *Great Friends!*
Edith Nesbit, *The Railway Children*
Eleanor H. Porter, *Pollyanna*
Anna Sewell, *Black Beauty*
Kenneth Grahame, *The Wind in the Willows*

Stage 2
Elizabeth Ferretti, *Dear Diary...*
Angela Tomkinson, *Loving London*
Mark Twain, *The Adventures of Tom Sawyer*
Mary Flagan, *The Egyptian Souvenir*
Maria Luisa Banfi, *A Faraway World*
Frances Hodgson Burnett, *The Secret Garden*
Robert Louis Stevenson, *Treasure Island*
Elizabeth Ferretti, *Adventure at Haydon Point*
William Shakespeare, *The Tempest*
Angela Tomkinson, *Enjoy New York*
Frances Hodgson Burnett, *Little Lord Fauntleroy*
Michael Lacey Freeman, *Egghead*
Michael Lacey Freeman, *Dot to Dot*
Silvana Sardi, *The Boy with the Red Balloon*
Silvana Sardi, *Scotland is Magic!*
Silvana Sardi, *Garpur: My Iceland*
Silvana Sardi, *Follow your Dreams*
Gabriele Rebagliati, *Naoko: My Japan*

Stage 3
Anna Claudia Ramos, *Expedition Brazil*
Charles Dickens, *David Copperfield*
Mary Flagan, *Val's Diary*
Maureen Simpson, *Destination Karminia*
Anonymous, *Robin Hood*
Jack London, *The Call of the Wild*
Louisa May Alcott, *Little Women*
Gordon Gamlin, *Allan: My Vancouver*